Whispered Prayers
for God's Ear

Whispered Prayers for God's Ear is a refreshing and uplifting book. The author's gift of blending God's Word with prayer and poetry is truly outstanding. Definitely a book to be added to my daily devotion.

Mike Kinnan
Aerospace Engineer

Whispered Prayers for God's Ear – A Collection of Poems is the integral use of Scripture in the crafting of poetry, giving each poem strength and authenticity. The gentle verses and pleasing rhymes are soothing to the soul. They embody firm assurance of the author's faith. The reader feels the sincerity of the praise, prayer, and experience, and takes joy from these "whispers" to God.

Mary-Ellen Grisham
Editor of *Eternal Ink,* **a Christian ezine**

I am amazed at how the author's prayers speak to me and are exactly what I need on a particular day. I am thankful she listens to God and spreads His love and counsel. I know you will enjoy reading and meditating on her latest book: *Whispered Prayers for God's Ear - A Collection of Poems.*

Marianne Schuler
Retired Member of Child Evangelism Fellowship

How refreshing to find a strong, Godly woman using her talents to glorify her Heavenly Father with beautiful Biblical-based poetry! *Whispered Prayers for God's Ear – A Collection of Poems,* offers encouragement to those seeking divine comfort and guidance in day-to-day decisions. The author's poems are born out of her deep trust in God's Word, and they minister to all ages.

Beth Coley
Group Leader in Bible Study Fellowship

The author has a unique way with words and has touched so many with her Biblical poetry. She helps others to understand and see the Light. Her creative lines are spoken with fervor and draw the reader into a new insightfulness and rendition of verses found in the Bible. She has mastered the art of making things extraordinary, exciting, and more meaningful. Thank you for your vignettes of joy.

Sharon Weeks
Good News Club Co-Administrator
Waterway Elementary School, Little River, SC

Whispered Prayers for God's Ear

A Collection of Poems

Kristine Stanton

Copyright @ 2021 Kristine Stanton
Whisper Prayers for God's Ear: A Collection of Poems

All rights reserved. No part of this publication may be reproduced or transmitted in any form or by any electronic or mechanical means including photo copying, recording, or any information storage and retrieval system now known or to be invented, without permission in writing from the publisher or the author.

Scripture quotations marked ASV are taken from the *American Standard Version*. This Bible is public domain in the United States. Biblegateway.com

Scripture quotations marked KJV are taken from the *King James Version*. This Bible is public domain in the United States. Biblegateway.com

Cover design: Bob Ousnamer
Cover photo: iStockphoto.com / guvendemir
Author's photograph: Used by permission, Lori Warren, photographer

ISBN: 978-1-953114-41-9
LCCN: 2021925370

Published by EA Books Publishing, a division of
Living Parables of Central Florida, Inc. a 501c3

EABooksPublishing.com

Dedication

To the Lord who blesses me each day, and to my parents, who exemplified the very essence of unconditional love.

Mom, I cherish you and your loving, gentle spirit. Thank you for having faith in me and always being an encourager. Know that I will be forever hugging your heart—You are a blessing I will treasure for the rest of my days.

To my dad, who has gone Home to rest. An endearing thanks for bringing laughter to my life and loving memories that will be alive in my heart forever.

To my children: Robert and Lindsay, and grandchildren: Jack, Ethan, Caroline, and Anna. Thank you for the joy you have brought to my life—I love each of you with all of my heart and soul.

Acknowledgements

Many thanks to Mike Kinnan and Kathleen Trasmondi Faust for your support in encouraging me to share my poems with others. You are both a blessing and an inspiration.

A special thanks to Janet Perez Eckles for her friendship, guidance, and wisdom. You are a refreshing ray of hope and sunshine to the hearts and souls of many.

Table Of Contents

Dedication and Acknowledgements 7
Who is God? 15
Whispered Prayers for God's Ear 17
Today's Blessings 18
I Witness the Lord's Glory 19
An Interview with God 20
Encouragement 22
Take Our Hands and Lead Us 23
The Potter and the Clay 24
Temptation 25
Another Soul was Won 26
Picture a World 28
Meet Me Where I Am 29
Life is an Adventure 30
Bless Me Lord 31
Sweet Seraphim of God 32
God with Me 33
Whirlwind 34
The Day – The Hour – The Minute 35
Wonder 36
The Lord's Creation 38
I Waited with Patience 39
The Loss of a Loved One 40
Shelter the Children 41
Calm 42
Think Before You Speak 43
Every Good and Perfect Gift 44
Grudges 45
God's Beautiful Creation 46
A Prayer for Children 47

Broken People	48
COVID-19	49
Why and When?	50
The Candy Cane	51
Help My Soul Repent	52
God of Hope	54
I Feel the Walls Around Me	55
The Lord Collects Our Tears	56
Prayer for a Friend	57
Puzzle Pieces	58
Diamonds on the Water	59
God's Love	60
The Race	61
Love and Faithfulness	62
Treasured Place	63
Where There Is	64
When My Foot is Slipping	65
Children	66
Seeds	67
Twinkling Stars	68
Love is Like a Flower	69
Eternal Peace	70
I Am Lord	71
Awaken and Rejoice	72
Rock the Children	73
The Armor of God	74
Honor Our Father	75
Christ Saves the Lost	76
Jesus Calms the Storms	78
The Word of God	79
Many Times I Wonder	80
Honoring Our Brave Soldiers	81
The Lord Most High	82
The Lord is My Fortress	83
A Tiny Babe Was Born	84

His Hands	86
My Eyes are Fixed on the Lord	87
Snow	88
Be Glad and Sing	90
You Made Me Brand New	91
I was an Imperfection	92
I was Knit by God	94
Man May Plan but God Directs	95
Cast Your Cares upon the Lord	96
God Began a Work in Me	97
The Lord Knows and Sees	98
Keep Yourself in God's Love	99
Glory Hallelujah Lord	100
I Poured My Heart Out	101
Why Have You Forsaken Me?	102
Forget the Past	103
A Special Gift	104
I Stand at the Door and Knock	105
Yesterday – Today – Tomorrow	106
Bring an End to Wickedness	107
Keep Your Tongue from Evil	108
Dwell Between His Shoulders	109
A Bouquet of Cheerful Joy	110
When a Man is a Slave	111
God's Plans for Me	112
Jealousy and Selfishness	113
When We Acknowledge Him	114
Listen for the Voice of God	115
The Lord Delights	116
Weary and Burdened	117
Creation Proclaims	118
Eyes You Granted Me	119
Our Savior's Gift	120
What Good Will It Be?	121
The Hand of God	122

Clothe Us.	124
Steadfast Feet	125
Bless the Children.	126
I Love Those Who Love Me.	127
Grace and Peace	128
Jesus Helps Those Tempted	129
I Cried to the Lord.	130
Many Will Come to Deceive.	131
The Lord is Our Shepherd.	132
Satan is a Prowler	133
Don't be Misled.	134
Implant Your Truth in Our Hearts	135
I Didn't Have a Choice	136
God's Peace.	137
I Wandered Through a Valley.	138
One Day in His Courts	139
Jesus Set Me Free	140
A Righteous Path	141
Be Still	142
Ask – Seek – Knock	143
Home.	144
Lead Us from the Evil One.	145
We Knock at the Door.	146
Yahweh Whispers to My Heart.	147
I Listened to the Quiet.	148
Bring Me to My Knees	149
Come One, Come All	150
The Day of the Lord	151
The Gift He Sent My Way	152
My Heart is Filled with Gratitude.	153
The Valley of Despair.	154
Turn Darkness to Light.	155
The Hands and Feet of Christ.	156
Commit to God.	157
Gathered Burdens	158

Dine with the Lord 159
God's Glory. 160
Equip Us with Your Armor. 161
He Knows What's in Your Heart 162
Quenching Rains. 163
The Seed of Loneliness. 164
I Lay My Heart Before You. 165
Amid the Quiet 166
Search My Heart and Soul 167
Rescued. 168
Seeds of Kindness. 170
Whispered Prayers 171
Prayer 172
Pray with All Your Heart 173

Who is God?

Who is God? Do you know, have you heard? God is the Creator of all things. He made the heavens and took a shapeless, empty form called Earth, filled it with light, water, dry land, and creatures of many kinds. In His image He created man and saw that this was good.

Who is God? "Hast thou not known? hast thou not heard, that the everlasting God, the LORD, the Creator of the ends of the earth, fainteth not, neither is weary? there is no searching of his understanding. He giveth power to the faint; and to them that have no might he increaseth strength . . . But they that wait upon the LORD shall renew their strength; they shall mount up with wings as eagles; they shall run, and not be weary; and they shall walk, and not faint," (Isaiah 40:28–29, 31, KJV).

Who is God? Do you know, have you heard? He is the great I AM. "It is he that sitteth upon the circle of the earth, and the inhabitants thereof are as grasshoppers; that stretcheth out the heavens as a curtain, and spreadeth them out as a tent to dwell in . . . To whom then will ye liken me, or shall I be equal? saith the Holy One. Lift up your eyes on high, and behold who hath created these things, that bringeth out their host by number: he calleth them all by names by the greatness of his might, for that he is strong in power; not one faileth," (Isaiah 40:22, 25–26, KJV).

Who is God? Do you know, have you heard? "The LORD is my rock, and my fortress, and my deliverer; my God, my strength, in whom I will trust; my buckler, and the horn of my salvation, and my high tower," (Psalm 18:2, KJV).

Who is God? Do you know, have you heard? He is our Heavenly Father whose "charity suffereth long, and is kind; charity envieth not; charity vaunteth not itself, is not puffed up, Doth not behave itself unseemly, seeketh not her own, is not easily provoked, thinketh no evil; Rejoiceth not in iniquity, but rejoiceth in the truth," (1 Corinthians 13:4–6, KJV). *Our Father's love embraces the heavens and all the earth—it never fails—it endures forever.*

Whispered Prayers for God's Ear

"I love the LORD, because he hath heard my voice
and my supplications.
Because he hath inclined his ear unto me,
therefore will I call upon him as long as I live."
(Psalm 116:1–2, KJV)

*Each whispered prayer that I lift up
is meant for my Lord's ear.
It comes from deep within my heart
and each one is sincere.
I thank the Lord for blessing me
with every prayer I pray
and praise Him for the mighty works
He does in me each day.*

"Blessed be God,
which hath not turned away my prayer,
nor his mercy from me . . .
I will "continue in prayer,
and watch in the same with thanksgiving."
(Psalm 66:20, Colossians 4:2, KJV)

Today's Blessings

"O LORD, thou art my God;
I will exalt thee, I will praise thy name;
for thou hast done wonderful things."
(Isaiah 25:1, KJV)

*Today I heard God whisper
so softly in my ear.
He told me that He loved me,
which caused my eyes to tear.*

*Today the good Lord hugged me,
my heart felt His embrace.
He took away my worries
and all the fears I face.*

*Today I saw God's blessings
through eyes He'd given me . . .
what I saw was so unlike
the things I'd known to be.*

I Witness the Lord's Glory

"I will praise the name of God with a song,
and will magnify him with thanksgiving."
(Psalm 69:30, KJV)

*As I gaze at the sunrise
what's staring back at me?
It's beauty God created
for all the world to see.*

*I witness the Lord's glory
ascending as it shines,
granting everyone on Earth
a gift that is divine.*

*The sleepy earth awakens
to yet another day
preparing for the blessings
the Lord will send its way.*

*I hear the creatures stirring
and singing to their King
a beautiful rendition,
a song is what they bring.*

*And as the day progresses
the earth prepares for sleep.
The moon reflects the sun's light
and shines upon God's sheep.*

*The stars begin to twinkle
and dance throughout the skies,
with wondrous light they sparkle
impressing watchful eyes.*

An Interview with God

*I had a lovely interview
with my sovereign God.
I answered several questions,
with each He gave a nod.*

*It started when my Father asked,
"Child, do you trust in Me?"
And from my heart I answered Him,
"I do, most certainly."*

*The Lord then asked about my faith
and if I knew His Son.
"The One who rescues and redeems?
O, yes, I know the One."*

*A smile then spread across His face
as He looked toward me.
God knew before I answered Him
that I spoke truthfully.*

*With every question that He asked
the Lord saw through my eyes . . .
the open windows to my soul
revealed if I'd told lies.*

*The good Lord knew my deepest thought,
'twas nothing I could hide.
I was an "open book," to Him,
it could not be denied.*

*He looked at me and then He said,
"Come, tell Me who I am."
"You are my God, the Lord Most High,
who sent His precious Lamb.*

You are the One who is most wise,
surpassing everything.
There's nothing that compares to You,
my sweet, beloved King.

You are the Lord who gives to me
His mercy, peace, and grace.
You have forgiven everyone,
all of the human race.

You are so faithful, loving, kind,
and give unselfishly.
You are my God who was and is,
and ever shall You be."

The Lord had one more question
to end the interview.
He gently took my hand and asked,
"Do you know I love you?"

I looked at Him with heart-felt joy,
so moved by what I'd heard.
My heart and soul began to soar,
awestruck by His grave words.

Beyond all measure I was touched
by love, my God endowed.
I softly whispered to the Lord,
with words I humbly vowed . . .

"I do acknowledge You, dear God,
and love You have for me.
I'm ever grateful for that love
You give so graciously."

'Twas then my Savior, Jesus Christ,
had joined the Lord and me . . .
We sat for several hours
in peace and harmony.

Encouragement

"Wherefore comfort yourselves together,
and edify one another, even as also ye do."
(1 Thessalonians 5:11, KJV)

*I pray that I encourage
the ones I meet each day
and lift them up in spirit
with everything I say.*

*Help me to achieve this task
O, Lord, my God above.
Please grant me words and actions
proclaiming Your pure love.*

Take Our Hands and Lead Us

*Take our hands and lead us
where gentle waters flow.
Wash us from within, Lord,
until our spirits glow.*

*Cleanse us of our misdeeds
and all our earthly woes.
Lead us, God in Heaven,
from paths where evil goes.*

*Fill our cups, dear Father,
until they overflow.
Anoint our heads with oil
and help our faith to grow.*

*Set for us a table
where we may dine and sing
and always dwell with You,
O, faithful, honored King.*

The Potter and the Clay

"But now, O LORD, thou are our father;
we are the clay, and thou our potter;
and we all are the work of thy hand."
(Isaiah 64:8, KJV)

*I was shattered pottery
until the Lord found me.
He fixed my broken pieces
so ever faithfully.*

*With diligence and fervor
God stretched and molded me.
He smoothed out all my rough spots
and gave me eyes to see . . .*

Temptation

"Watch and pray, that ye enter not into temptation . . .
The thief cometh not, but for to steal, and to kill, and to destroy."
(Matthew 26:41, John 10:10, KJV)

*Temptation is the devil's work
that tries to find its way
into each and every heart
to lure mankind astray.*

*It lurks around in many forms
in search of young and old.
This thief will steal the souls of all
who let their souls be sold.*

So . . .

*Rebuke temptation when it strikes,
don't let it have its way.
Just fix your eyes upon the Lord
and you won't go astray.*

"The LORD knoweth
how to deliver the godly out of temptations."
(2 Peter 2:9, KJV)

Another Soul was Won

*I never met a stranger
my Father did not know,
but once I met a stranger
who knew not God but woe.*

*His heart was very heavy
and tarnished by his sins.
He thought that no one loved him,
as darkness lived within.*

*I listened to his story
as tears fell from my eyes.
This man had suffered greatly
and knew the reasons why.*

*He made several choices
that laced his heart with sin,
causing friends and family
to walk away from him.*

*'Twas then I turned to face him
and earnestly I said,
"Please know you've been forgiven
of sin, and life you've led."*

*I told him he'd be washed clean
and given a fresh start
if he'd turn to Jesus Christ
and ask Him in his heart.*

*After several minutes,
this man got on his knees.
He asked the Lord's forgiveness . . .
"Forgive me, will You please?"*

*Uplifted by God's glory
and mercy of His Son,
he knelt before the Father
and another soul was won.*

"Therefore if any man be in Christ,
he is a new creature: old things are passed away;
behold, all things are become new."
(2 Corinthians 5:17, KJV)

Picture a World

"I am the LORD. If ye walk in my statutes,
and keep my commandments, and do them . . .
I will give peace in the land, and ye shall lie down,
and none shall make you afraid:
and I will rid evil beasts out of the land,
neither shall the sword go through your land.
And ye shall chase your enemies,
and they shall fall before you by the sword."
(Leviticus 26:2–3, 6–7, KJV)

Picture a world not tempted by sin,
no one living in a place that's dim.

Picture a world surrounded by peace,
no brutal wars, they've all come to cease.

Picture a world with absence of crime,
a place to live with no stressful times.

Picture a world with no more disease,
an end to pain, all living with ease.

Picture a world that's down on its knees,
humbly praying to One no one sees.

Picture the Lord hearing those prayers,
Almighty God, the good Lord who cares.

Picture the world all pristine and clean,
saved by Jesus—a world that's redeemed . . .

Meet Me Where I Am

"A man's pride shall bring him low:
but honour shall uphold the humble in spirit."
(Proverbs 29:23, KJV)

*Please meet me where I am, dear Lord,
I'm lost and all alone.
I've traveled very far, You know,
so far away from home.*

*I know I've been estranged from You
and did things on my own.
I did not listen when You spoke
and now I must atone.*

*I do confess that I've been wrong
and want to change my ways.
I'm in a place that I don't like
and do not want to stay.*

*I'm ready to give up my pride
and ask You grant me grace.
I want to live a faithful life
with all my past erased.*

"I will not leave you comfortless:
I will come to you."
(John 14:18, KJV)

Life is an Adventure

"Trust in the LORD with all thine heart;
and lean not unto thine own understanding.
In all thy ways acknowledge him,
and he shall direct thy paths."
(Proverbs 3:5–6, KJV)

Energy's flowing, can you feel it within?
O, life's an adventure about to begin.
Now, fasten your seatbelt and look straight ahead.
Don't ever look back, there is nothing to dread.

The ride may be bumpy, but that is okay,
you're never in danger when God leads the way.
Obey His instructions, please listen to Him,
and He'll steer your ride far away from all sin.

The ride may continue to go up and down,
through peaks and through valleys, where faith can be found.
Please keep your eyes open and fixed on the Lord,
and you'll be amazed as He opens closed doors.

The doors may be many, or they may be few.
God will unlock them—He'll unlock them for you.
Have faith in the good Lord and reach for His hand.
Trust He'll protect you, and the ride will be grand.

Bless Me Lord

"But Jesus beheld them, and said unto them,
With men this is impossible;
but with God all things are possible."
(Matthew 19:26, KJV)

*Please bless me, Lord, this very day
and draw me close to You.
Your love is what I need right now,
You know what I've been through.*

*I feel alone and want to cry,
I'm frightened and it shows.
I look around for help, dear God,
I'm lost and feeling low.*

*Come help me find my way, sweet Lord,
and lift me from despair.
I know all things are possible
for You are everywhere.*

*My Lord, my God, I love You so
and praise You faithfully.
With all my heart I thank You, Lord,
for loving all of me.*

Sweet Seraphim of God

*Sing to me a lullaby,
sweet seraphim of God.
Take me to a peaceful place
where no mankind has trod.*

*Carry me upon your wings
and keep me safe each day.
Guard my heart and guard my soul . . .
with faith and hope I pray.*

God with Me

"Peace I leave with you, my peace I give unto you:
not as the world giveth, give I unto you.
Let not your heart be troubled, neither let it be afraid."
(John 14:27, KJV)

*While sitting on the sand
and gazing out to sea,
my soul had come to rest
with God there next to me.*

*The sun began to shine
as darkness turned to light.
'Twas then God touched my heart
and all my fears took flight.*

*The good Lord gave me peace,
this gift He gave to me,
and all my troubled cares
then drifted out to sea.*

Whirlwind

"God is our refuge and strength,
a very present help in trouble.
Therefore will not we fear."
(Psalm 46:1–2, KJV)

*'Round and 'round the world does turn—
a roller coaster ride.
Spinning, moving very fast,
there is no place to hide.*

*Twisting, turning, aimlessly
around so many bends
the ride continues onward,
it seems to never end.*

*Screaming, crying, calling out
with tears and fearful cries.
Helpless feelings take control
with breathless, weary sighs.*

*Then a mighty voice is heard
from very deep inside.
It tells me to be still, with love,
"I'm right here by your side."*

*The ride has stopped, fear has gone,
they've each been placed on hold.
Calming peace then captures me
and stills my inner soul.*

*God has come to rescue me,
He's come to set me free,
from the whirlwind spinning 'round
that caught and carried me.*

The Day – The Hour – The Minute

"But of that day and hour knoweth no man,
no, not the angels of heaven,
but my Father only."
(Matthew 24:36, KJV)

*The day, hour, or minute
of Jesus Christ's return
is not known by man nor beast—
a time they've yet to learn.*

Wonder

"In the beginning God created the heaven and the earth . . .
And God saw every thing that he had made,
and, behold, it was very good."
(Genesis 1:1, 31, KJV)

*Have you ever stopped to wonder
how all things came to be
and in those times of wonder,
did you notice, did you see . . .*

*The beauty of Creation
that surrounds both you and me,
the clouds up in the heavens
and the roaring, rolling sea?*

*The moon, the stars, the sun that shines,
the earth beneath your feet,
the songs you hear at break of day
by trilling birds that tweet?*

*Did the fragrances at springtime
from blooms with lovely scents
embrace the air with sweetness,
precious gifts the good Lord sent?*

*Have your eyes beheld the beauty
that autumn colors bring
as orange, red, and yellow leaves
cloak branches where they cling?*

*Have you caught the hint of raindrops
'fore they were Heaven sent?
Did you notice how the air stirred
as rains made their descent?*

Have you listened to the quiet
as snow falls to the ground?
Did you feel the peace of God
and give ear to other sounds?

As you ponder all these questions,
please know that God above
created all you witnessed
with His wisdom, grace, and love.

And though you do not see Him
know the Lord will always be.
He was, and is the great I AM
who lives in you and me.

The Lord's Creation

"The heavens declare the glory of God;
and the firmament sheweth his handywork."
(Psalm 19:1, KJV)

*I climbed atop a mountain
and looked out o'er the land.
I saw the Lord's Creation
and beauty He had planned.*

*In all His wondrous splendor
God gave the earth to man
and let him live upon it
to govern all the land.*

*I stood there in amazement
by what my eyes could see.
My heart was captivated
as peace encircled me.*

*The beauty that I witnessed
no words could quite explain.
'Twas the handy work of God,
the mighty King who reigns.*

*Humbly I bowed down to Him,
with fervor I did pray
to thank the Lord in Heaven
for this amazing day.*

I Waited with Patience

"I waited patiently for the LORD;
and he inclined unto me, and heard my cry.
He brought me up also out of an horrible pit,
out of the miry clay, and set my feet upon a rock,
and established my goings.
And he hath put a new song in my mouth,
even praise unto our God."
(Psalm 40:1–3, KJV)

*I waited with patience
for God to help me.
He saw my affliction
and heard all my pleas.*

*God lifted me up
from the pit of despair,
a place I had traveled
that led me nowhere.*

*He steadied my feet
on a path with firm ground
and made my heart sing
for the new life I'd found.*

The Loss of a Loved One

"The LORD is nigh unto them that are of a broken heart;
and saveth such as be of a contrite spirit."
(Psalm 34:18, KJV)

Lord,

*Many hearts are suffering
the loss of a loved one.
Bless and soothe each grieving soul
before the day is done.*

*Immerse them in Your goodness,
embrace them in Your peace,
bring them to a tranquil place
and make the hurting cease.*

*Relieve them of their sorrow
and in the days ahead
comfort them with mercy, Lord,
and keep their spirits fed.*

*Hold them in Your arms, dear God,
and wipe their tears away.
Please let them know their loved one
is in Your care each day.*

Shelter the Children

"Deliver me, O LORD, from the evil man:
preserve me from the violent man."
(Psalm 140:1, KJV)

Lord,

*We acknowledge all the children
and love their openness.
Please shelter them beneath Your wing
and calm their restlessness.*

*Protect them from the evil one
who searches for his prey.
Don't let them lose their innocence,
watch over them each day.*

Calm

"He maketh the storm a calm,
so that the waves thereof are still."
(Psalm 107:29, KJV)

*Forceful winds may bluster
and ocean waves may roar,
but Christ's majestic voice
can calm them all for sure.*

Think Before You Speak

"Whosoever shall smite thee on thy right cheek,
turn to him the other also."
(Matthew 5:39, KJV)

*Be one who is forgiving
and turn the other cheek.
Be wise with words and actions
and think before you speak.*

"A time to keep silence, and a time to speak."
(Ecclesiastes 3:7, KJV)

Every Good and Perfect Gift

"Every good gift and every perfect gift
is from above,
and cometh down from the Father of lights."
(James 1:17, KJV)

*Baskets of gladness
each woven with lace,
gifts from the Father
perfected with grace.*

*Bouquets of mercy,
warm blankets of love,
joyfully knitted
by Yahweh above.*

*Ribbons of patience
entwined with God's peace,
blessings abounding
not ever to cease.*

*Gifts from the Father,
the Father of Lights,
are made with His love
and make the world bright.*

Grudges

"Thou shalt not avenge,
nor bear any grudge against the children
of thy people."
(Leviticus 19:18, KJV)

*When a grudge invades your heart
it weaves a web of sin,
and your soul becomes ensnared
as darkness grows within.*

*Tangled webs intrigue revenge,
the two walk hand-in-hand,
staking claim to evil whims
that spread at their command.*

So . . .

*When a grudge takes hold of you
don't let it have its way.
Release it to the Father
and then just walk away.*

*For we should love our neighbors
as God loves you and me.
And we should not hold grudges . . .
forgive, and set them free.*

"Thou shalt love thy neighbour as thyself."
(Leviticus 19:18, KJV)

God's Beautiful Creation

"Thus the heavens and the earth were finished,
and all the host of them . . .
And God saw every thing that he had made,
and, behold, it was very good."
(Genesis 2:1, 1:31, KJV)

*In all of God's Creation
pure beauty can be found
and if you take a moment
you'll see it's all around.*

*From high above the mountains
to valleys down below,
from stars up in the heavens
to the moon's reflective glow.*

*From depths of mighty oceans
to glorious skies above,
God shares all His Creation
and showers us with love.*

"Bless the LORD, O my soul . . .
Who laid the foundations of the earth . . .
O LORD my God, thou art very great."
(Psalm 104:1, 5, 1, KJV)

A Prayer for Children

*We pray for children in this world
who know bloodshed, not peace.
Please gather them to You, dear Lord,
and make the wars all cease.*

*We pray for children in this world
who live in fear each day.
Please hug their hearts to ease their fears
and wipe their tears away.*

*We pray for children in this world
who suffer from abuse.
Please rescue them from criminals
who harm them through misuse.*

*We pray for children in this world
that each one comes to You.
Please heal their hearts and help them share
Your glory and Good News.*

Broken People

"Shew me thy ways, O LORD; teach me thy paths.
Lead me in thy truth, and teach me:
for thou art the God of my salvation;
on thee do I wait all the day. Remember,
O LORD, thy tender mercies
and thy lovingkindnesses; for they have been ever of old.
Remember not the sins of my youth, nor my transgressions:
according to thy mercy remember thou me
for thy goodness' sake, O LORD . . .
Look upon mine affliction and my pain;
and forgive all my sins."
(Psalm 25:4–7, 18, KJV)

We come as broken people
and kneel before You, Lord.
We're sorry for our weakness
and evil we've explored.

We call on You, dear Father,
and ask You to forgive
the wrongful things we've done
and for the lives we live.

Show us how to change, O Lord,
and live Your will, not ours.
Lead us with Your faithfulness,
truth, and mighty power.

COVID-19

"Now when the sun was setting,
all they that had any sick with divers diseases
brought them unto him;
and he laid his hands on every one of them,
and healed them."
(Luke 4:40, KJV)

*The world is infected
and many have died.
The virus is spreading,
there's no place to hide.*

*O, spare us this sickness
that's left us undone.
Please come to our aid, Lord,
and heal everyone.*

Why and When?

"Cease from anger, and forsake wrath:
fret not thyself in any wise to do evil."
(Psalm 37:8, KJV)

*Why do people want to hurt
other human beings?
Don't they see the harm they cause,
are their eyes unseeing?*

*When did all the hatred start,
just how did it begin?
When will all the anger stop
that leads the world to sin?*

*When will all the fighting end,
when will the world know peace?
When will evil leave this world,
O, will it ever cease?*

*The answers to these questions
are only known by One
who observes and knows the world
and what mankind has done.*

"For evildoers shall be cut off: but those that wait upon the LORD,
they shall inherit the earth.
For yet a little while, and the wicked shall not be."
(Psalm 37:9–10, KJV)

*Those who wait upon the Lord
and do what pleases Him
won't be led upon a path
that leads mankind to sin.*

*And someday in the future
the wicked will not be,
then all on Earth shall come to live
in peace and harmony.*

The Candy Cane

*A candy cane turned upside down
forms the letter "J"
and if you add "E-S-U-S,"
what does this word say?*

"JESUS"

*The cane looks like a shepherd's crook
when turned the other way.
It's used to herd the flock of sheep
so they won't go astray.*

Help My Soul Repent

"And they went out,
and preached that men should repent."
(Mark 6:12, KJV)

*One day I met a woman
with kind and loving eyes,
who had a gentle spirit
and was extremely wise.*

*Her face showed signs of aging,
her lovely hair was gray.
She wore a knitted black shawl
and tattered red beret.*

*Her hands were slightly shaking
while leaning on her cane.
She walked with a pronounced limp
that showed she was in pain.*

*Yet, this woman smiled
with happiness and grace.
She spoke to me with kindness
as sunrays kissed her face.*

*She told me of a Savior
whose name was Jesus Christ,
and how He'd lived among us
and what He sacrificed.*

*She called Him her Redeemer,
One sent by God above,
who changed her life forever
with patience, grace, and love.*

*This precious, gentle woman
then held my hand and prayed.
She asked if I knew Jesus
and ransom He had paid.*

*I said I did not know Him
but truly wanted to
know this man named Jesus Christ.
"What did I need to do?"*

*'Twas then this woman led me
to Jesus Christ, our Lord.
I asked for His forgiveness.
O, humbly I implored . . .*

*And at that very moment,
I thought, "What can this be?"
My heart and soul awakened
as peace encircled me.*

"Repent ye therefore, and be converted,
that your sins may be blotted out,
when the times of refreshing
shall come from the presence of the Lord."
(Acts 3:19, KJV)

*My Jesus, Lord and Savior,
I'm grateful that You sent
this kind and Godly woman
to help my soul repent.*

God of Hope

"Your Father knoweth
what things ye have need of, before ye ask him."
(Matthew 6:8, KJV)

*The God of Hope fulfills our dreams
and meets our every need.
He fills each void so there are none
for those who are redeemed.*

"And now, Lord, what wait I for?
my hope is in thee."
(Psalm 39:7, KJV)

I Feel the Walls Around Me

*I feel the walls around me,
they're slowly moving in.
I cannot push or stop them
from crushing me within.*

*I've looked to You for guidance
and thought You were not there.
I've learned that it was me, Lord,
Who hid and went nowhere.*

*I'm frightened and alone, God,
and don't know what to do.
O, help me to escape, Lord,
please help me see this through.*

*I need to see the footprints
that Jesus left behind.
Please show me where they are, Lord,
they're very hard to find.*

*I pray my eyes be opened
to see the path ahead,
the one You chose for me, Lord,
and not the one I dread.*

*I'd be forever grateful
if Jesus took the lead.
I'd follow in His footsteps
to bypass evil deeds.*

The Lord Collects Our Tears

"Thou tellest my wanderings:
put thou my tears into thy bottle."
(Psalm 56:8, KJV)

*The Lord has heard you crying
in the darkness of the night
and He's seen each tear that's shed,
they are precious in His sight.*

*Although you may not know it,
Yahweh gathers every tear
and saves them in a bottle,
where they're kept year-after-year.*

*Your tears have been recorded
in the Good Book that He keeps.
Each one has its importance,
every single one you weep.*

Prayer for a Friend

*I said a little prayer for you,
a special prayer, my friend.
I asked the Lord to give you hugs,
sweet ones that never end.*

Puzzle Pieces

*Our lives are puzzle pieces
and each one has its place.
God brings them all together
and blesses them with grace.*

*Though some may have rough edges,
God uses every one.
He takes and molds these pieces
until His work is done.*

*It's when the Lord is finished,
this perfect masterpiece,
all parts will fit together
with harmony and peace.*

Diamonds on the Water

*Diamonds on the water,
all sparkling in the sun,
are messages from God
for each and every one.*

*Although they do not speak,
no sound is ever heard,
they tell of our Lord's love
without a single word.*

*God sends these special gifts
for everyone to view—
sweet messages from God
that offer His peace too.*

God's Love

"Love suffereth long, *and* is kind; love envieth not;
love vaunteth not itself, is not puffed up,
doth not behave itself unseemly,
seeketh not its own, is not provoked,
taketh not account of evil;
rejoiceth not in unrighteousness,
but rejoiceth with the truth;
beareth all things, believeth all things,
hopeth all things, endureth all things.
Love never faileth."
(1 Corinthians 13:4–8, ASV)

*God's love is patient, mighty, and strong;
it holds no grudges even when wronged.
Love is not jealous, it is divine;
it's never ending, loyal, and kind.
Love isn't selfish, haughty, or rude;
it's not demanding, nor is it crude.
Love is respectful, truthful, and pure.
The Lord gives to all a love that endures.*

The Race

"Know ye not that they which run in a race run all,
but one receiveth the prize? So run, that ye may obtain.
And every man that striveth for the mastery
is temperate in all things.
Now they do it to obtain a corruptible crown;
but we an incorruptible.
I therefore so run, not as uncertainly; so fight I,
not as one that beateth the air: But I keep under my body,
and bring it into subjection: lest that by any means,
when I have preached to others, I myself should be a castaway."
(1 Corinthians 9:24-27, KJV)

Lord,

*Guide me to the path that's carved
with footprints Jesus made.
Take my hand and lead me where
I'll journey unafraid.*

*Give me speed to outrun sin
that's known to tie me down.
Help me shed what hinders me
and win the lasting crown.*

*Bless me as I run this race
and keep me safe from harm.
Let me see Your shining face
and strong, sustaining arms.*

*Be there at the finish line,
encourage me to run,
and I will run with faith and trust
until the race is done.*

Love and Faithfulness

"Let not kindness and truth forsake thee:
Bind them about thy neck;
Write them upon the tablet of thy heart."
(Proverbs 3:3, ASV)

*I pray God binds His kindness
and truth around my neck
so that I won't lose these gifts
that keep my heart in check.*

Treasured Place

*'Twas very long ago
I found a treasured place
concealed within God's peace
and His amazing grace.*

*He led me to this spot,
a place with tranquil grounds.
I closed my eyes to rest
and felt no longer bound.*

*I had no need for want,
I felt refreshed and whole.
Still waters washed me clean
as God restored my soul.*

"The LORD is my shepherd; I shall not want.
He maketh me to lie down in green pastures:
he leadeth me beside the still waters.
He restoreth my soul."
(Psalm 23:1-3, KJV)

*I'll never be in want
while Jesus is with me.
He stills my heart and soul
while I rest peacefully.*

Where There Is . . .

Where there is kindness, there is compassion
Where there is laughter, there is joy
Where there is truth, there is honor
Where there is trust, there is belief
Where there is prayer, there is communion
Where there is love, there is God

When My Foot is Slipping

"When I said, My foot slippeth;
thy mercy, O LORD, held me up.
In the multitude of my thoughts within me
thy comforts delight my soul."
(Psalm 94:18-19, KJV)

*Lord, when my foot is slipping
I lift my voice to You,
and when my soul is anxious
it's You that I go to.*

*You give me strength with mercy
and as I face my fears
You gently grasp my hand, Lord,
and calmly draw me near.*

*My soul delights in You, God.
You're always here for me.
O, without You, my sweet Lord,
I'd wander aimlessly.*

Children

"And a little child shall lead them."
(Isaiah 11:6, ASV)

*The hopes and dreams of all children
are seen through innocent eyes.
They're forever asking questions,
their favorite one is "why?"*

*When they're face-to-face with danger
delight overcomes their fears.
They view all things with excitement
and laugh 'til their eyes fill with tears.*

*Their days are filled with adventure
waiting for them to explore.
They open their eyes each morning
with plans to head out the door.*

*Children are sweet and trusting
and watched by angels, with love.
They're born without ever asking
and blessed by the Lord above.*

Seeds

"The sower soweth the word. And these are they by the way side,
where the word is sown; but when they have heard,
Satan cometh immediately, and taketh away the word
that was sown in their hearts" . . .
And "they which are sown among thorns;
such as hear the word, And the cares of this world,
and the deceitfulness of riches,
and the lusts of other things entering in,
choke the word, and it becometh unfruitful.
And these are they which are sown on good ground;
such as hear the word, and receive it, and bring forth fruit,
some thirtyfold, some sixty, and some an hundred."
(Mark 4:14–15, 18–20, KJV)

Blooming flowers are from God,
they sprout from tiny seeds.
Some grow strong, and some grow tall;
some are choked by weeds.

Those who strive to live for God
are fed by Him each day,
and those who live among the weeds
grow parched and wilt away.

Twinkling Stars

"Lift up your eyes on high,
and behold who hath created these things,
that bringeth out their host by number:
he calleth them all by names
by the greatness of his might,
for that he is strong in power;
not one faileth."
(Isaiah 40:26, KJV)

*Twinkling stars shine vividly
throughout the skies at night
and Earth becomes a witness
to visions of God's light.*

*They glitter and they sparkle
around a well-lit moon
presenting the appearance
they're waltzing to a tune.*

*While dancing in the heavens,
so high up in the skies,
stars give a grand performance
before our very eyes.*

*And one-by-one they're counted
by God, who named each one—
the ones that dance before us
before each night is done.*

Love is Like a Flower

"And some fell among thorns,
and the thorns grew up, and choked it,
and it yielded no fruit."
(Mark 4:7, KJV)

*Love is like a flower,
it starts from planted seeds.
It will grow when nourished
and die when choked by weeds.*

Eternal Peace

"Depart from evil, and do good . . .
And let the peace of God rule in your hearts,
to the which also ye are called in one body;
and be ye thankful."
(Psalm 34:14, Colossians 3:15, KJV)

Eternal peace is of the Lord
when we turn from sin.
He places it within our hearts
when we live in Him.

So . . .

Withdraw from evil and do good,
let peace direct your heart,
for you were called to be in Christ—
a gift that God imparts.

I Am Lord

"And God said unto Moses,
I AM THAT I AM."
(Exodus 3:14, KJV)

O, be it known that I AM LORD,
Creator of all things.
I know the hearts and souls of all
and what each day will bring.

Come trust in Me, the Lord your God,
I know the chosen Way
and I've designed a path for you
to follow every day.

Awaken and Rejoice

"Sing unto God, sing praises to his name:
extol him that rideth upon the heavens
by his name JAH, and rejoice before him."
(Psalm 68:4, KJV)

*Awaken to the morning sun
with happiness and glee.
O, look around with open eyes,
get down on bended knee.*

*Rejoice in Him who rides the clouds,
sing out and praise our King.
Revere the Lord with love and grace,
extol Him as you sing.*

Rock the Children

Dear Lord,

*Rock the children in Your arms
and take away their fears.
Please protect their innocence
and wipe away their tears.*

*Pick them up when they fall down
and kiss their wounded hearts.
Teach them what they need to know
before the battles start.*

*Give them strength when they are weak,
prepare them with Your Word.
Be their Rock, Almighty God,
and let Your voice be heard.*

The Armor of God

"Be strong in the Lord . . . Put on the whole armor of God,
that ye may be able to stand against the wiles of the devil . . .
Stand therefore, having your loins girt about with truth,
and having on the breastplate of righteousness;
And your feet shod with the preparation of the gospel of peace;
Above all, taking the shield of faith,
wherewith ye shall be able to quench all the fiery darts
of the wicked.
And take the helmet of salvation, and the sword of the Spirit,
which is the word of God."
(Ephesians 6:10–11, 14–17, KJV)

As soldiers we march with faith in the Lord.
We're armed with His Word, that's known as God's Sword.
Adorned with the Truth that's tied at our waist
we go to battle with undaunted haste.

We're given a shield, delivered with grace,
to fend off evil and harm that we face.
A breastplate is placed upon every chest.
It's granted with love and God's righteousness.

We wear a helmet that rests on our heads—
a gift from Jesus, who rose from the dead.
Our feet are fitted with footwear that lead
and bring us to those lost and in need.

Honor Our Father

"My little children,
let us not love in word,
neither in tongue;
but in deed and in truth."
(1 John 3:18, KJV)

Honor the Father in all that you do.
Hurt not your brothers as they have hurt you.
Be kind in action, in word, and in deed.
Give glory to God and sow all good seeds.

Christ Saves the Lost

"For the Son of man is come to seek and to save
that which was lost."
(Luke 19:10, KJV)

*I walked upon a path
where I didn't want to be.
O, darkness was the friend
that trapped and misled me.*

*I stayed there for a while
in that dark, dreary place,
just crying out in fear
as tears streamed down my face.*

*I dropped down to my knees
and prayed to God I'd see
so I could find my way
through darkness blinding me.*

*It's then I heard a voice
from deep within my heart.
The voice expressed His grief
that we had grown apart.*

*I begged His forgiveness
and asked that He help me.
He said He'd heard my call
and came to set me free.*

And at that very moment . . .

*The darkness had diminished
and then my eyes could see
that Jesus was the friend
who came to rescue me.*

Jesus Calms the Storms

"And when he was entered into a ship, his disciples followed him.
And, behold, there arose a great tempest in the sea,
insomuch that the ship was covered with the waves:
but he was asleep.
And his disciples came to him, and awoke him, saying,
Lord, save us: we perish. And he saith unto them,
Why are ye fearful, O ye of little faith?
Then he arose, and rebuked the winds and the sea;
and there was a great calm."
(Matthew 8:23–26, KJV)

There are storms that come upon us
that reach our very core,
with flashing scenes of lightning bolts
and sounds of thunderous roars.

Now, should those storms that hem us in
turn brutal and untamed,
Christ Jesus is the One to call—
call Jesus by His name.

And as we place our trust in Him,
with all the storms we face,
He'll prove to be the calming voice
that tames each storm with grace.

The Word of God

"For the word of God is quick, and powerful,
and sharper than any twoedged sword,
piercing even to the dividing asunder
of soul and spirit,
and of the joints and marrow,
and is a discerner of the thoughts
and intents of the heart."
(Hebrews 4:12, KJV)

The Word is sharper than a sword
that penetrates the soul
and it will judge our thoughts and deeds
then work to make us whole.

Many Times I Wonder

*So many times I wonder
how Yahweh came to be.
O, how was He created
and why did He make me?*

*I do not know the answers
but some day He'll tell me.
It's when I get to Heaven
that I will know and see.*

Honoring Our Brave Soldiers

*We gather together to honor
the memories of those who've died,
the ones who defended our country,
the ones we esteem with great pride.*

*We salute these men and these women
who have given unselfishly.
Because of their brave dedication
we live in a Land that is free.*

The Lord Most High

"He that dwelleth in the secret place of the most High
shall abide under the shadow of the Almighty . . .
Thou shalt not be afraid for the terror by night;
nor for the arrow that flieth by day;
Nor for the pestilence that walketh in darkness . . .
Because thou hast made the LORD, which is my refuge,
even the most High, thy habitation;
There shall no evil befall thee . . .
For he shall give his angels charge over thee,
to keep thee in all thy ways.
They shall bear thee up in their hands,
lest thou dash thy foot against a stone."
(Psalm 91:1, 5–6, 9–12, KJV)

*If you make the Lord Most High
your home, your dwelling place,
He will shelter you from harm
and darkness you might face.*

*You'll not dread the dead of night
nor darts that fly by day,
you'll not fear the deadly plagues
that devastate their prey.*

So . . .

*If you need the Lord Most High
He'll come to your rescue.
He will send His messengers
to guard and lift you, too.*

*In their charge they'll bear you up
to keep you safe and sound
and keep your foot from striking
the stones found on the ground.*

The Lord is My Fortress

"But the LORD is my defense;
and my God is the rock of my refuge."
(Psalm 94:22, KJV)

The Lord is my Rock
and always shall be.
He is my Defense
who battles for me.

A Tiny Babe Was Born

"And there were in the same country
shepherds abiding in the field,
keeping watch over their flock by night.
And, lo, the angel of the Lord came upon them,
and the glory of the Lord shone round about them:
and they were sore afraid.
And the angel said unto them, Fear not:
for, behold, I bring you good tidings of great joy,
which shall be to all people. For unto you is born this day
in the city of David a Saviour, which is Christ the Lord.
And this shall be a sign unto you;
Ye shall find the babe wrapped
in swaddling clothes, lying in a manger."
(Luke 2:8–12, KJV)

So long ago in Bethlehem
a tiny babe was born.
He lay upon a bed of hay,
in cloths He was adorned.

This humble scene was glorious
as angels gathered 'round.
'Twas then a star shone o'er the earth . . .
a newborn King was crowned.

Now, shepherds in the fields below
had witnessed this bright star.
It's then an angel came to them,
an angel from afar.

He told them, "Do not be afraid
I bring you news of joy.
A Savior has been born this day,
a blessed baby boy."

"And suddenly there was with the angel
a multitude of the heavenly host
praising God, and saying,
Glory to God in the highest,
and on earth peace, good will toward men."
(Luke 2:13–14, KJV)

O, glory be to God on High,
good will, and peace on Earth.
Come gather 'round to celebrate
the Christ-child's sacred birth.

His Hands

"For the LORD is a great God,
and a great King above all gods.
In his hand are the deep places of the earth:
the strength of the hills is his also.
The sea is his, and he made it:
and his hands formed the dry land."
(Psalm 95:3–5, KJV)

'Tis Thee, wise Creator,
who formed the dry land
and the depths of the earth
are all in Thy hand.

O, Thou art the Maker
of vast, mighty seas
and peaks of all mountains
were fashioned by Thee.

The skies in the heavens
and all living things
belong to Thee, Yahweh,
All-Powerful King.

My Eyes are Fixed on the Lord

"Mine eyes are ever toward the LORD;
for he shall pluck my feet out of the net."
(Psalm 25:15, KJV)

*I can't be distracted by trouble
when my eyes are fixed on the One
who leads me from sin and from sorrow
and shows me how battles are won.*

*I'm embraced by songs of victory
when I walk in faith with the Lord.
He shows me the places where glory
is honored and can't be ignored.*

Snow

'Twas a cold winter's night,
no creature was heard.
Snow fell from the heavens,
winds blustered and stirred.

The rooftops were covered
and the earth below
by beautiful blankets
of white driven snow.

And the moon and the stars
shed lights from above
as the Lord's wondrous peace
touched the earth with love.

When the dark of the night
moved on to daylight
the earth had awakened
to a dazzling sight.

All the blustery winds
had now settled down
as snow filled the heavens,
not making a sound.

The children awakened
with eyes all aglow
and ran to their windows
to see the white snow.

Alive with excitement
they quickly got dressed
with hats, scarves, and mittens,
'Twas no time for rest.

*The children all headed
out-of-doors to play.
With sleds, skates, and snowballs
they had fun all day . . .*

*The sweet sound of laughing
reached Heaven above
and the Lord looked at each
with gladness and love.*

Be Glad and Sing

"Make a joyful noise unto the LORD,
all ye lands.
Serve the LORD with gladness:
come before his presence with singing."
(Psalm 100:1–2, KJV)

*May all the earth be glad and sing
before the presence of our King.*

You Made Me Brand New

"Therefore if any man be in Christ,
he is a new creature:
old things are passed away;
behold, all things are become new."
(2 Corinthians 5:17, KJV)

*Heavenly Father, You made me brand new.
I'm not the same since I found You.*

I was an Imperfection

"And he said unto her, Thy sins are forgiven."
(Luke 7:48, KJV)

*I was an imperfection
just sitting on a shelf.
I chose to climb and hide there
to be all by myself.*

*But then a kindly stranger
appeared and noticed me.
He saw that I was lonely,
'twas not a place to be.*

*He looked at me with sadness
and eyes of tenderness
then gently did He lift me
to view my brokenness.*

*He saw my imperfections
and did not turn away.
Instead, He smiled sweetly
in such a caring way.*

*I felt ashamed and tarnished
by things I'd said and done;
the sins I carried with me
I'd not told anyone.*

*And then this gentle stranger
had said these words to me,
"I forgive all of your past
and came to set you free."*

He said His name was Jesus,
and He was sent to me,
to fix my broken pieces
and restore my dignity.

And now . . .

I'm no longer broken pieces
hiding out upon a shelf.
Since this stranger came and found me
I am not all by myself.

All my pieces have been mended
and my heart sings out with glee
'cause this man who was a stranger
has become a friend to me.

I Was Knit by God

"For thou hast possessed my reins:
thou hast covered me in my mother's womb.
I will praise thee; for I am fearfully and wonderfully made:
marvelous are thy works; and that my soul knoweth right well.
My substance was not hid from thee, when I was made in secret,
and curiously wrought in the lowest parts of the earth.
Thine eyes did see my substance, yet being unperfect;
and in thy book all my members were written,
which in continuance were fashioned,
when as yet there was none of them."
(Psalm 139:13–16, KJV)

I was knit by God above,
each stitch was laced with grace and love.
He wove me in my mother's womb,
a seed I was that came to bloom.
And all the days ordained for me
God wrote before I came to be.

Man May Plan but God Directs

"A man's heart deviseth his way:
but the LORD directeth his steps."
(Proverbs 16:9, KJV)

*A man may plan the course he takes
but God directs the steps he makes.*

Cast Your Cares upon the Lord

"Cast thy burden upon the LORD,
and he shall sustain thee:
he shall never suffer the righteous to be moved."
(Psalm 55:22, KJV)

Lord,

*We cast our cares upon You
with hope and faith and trust
that You will take our burdens
and all that is unjust.*

*Come help us soar like eagles
and never let us fall.
With kindness, grace, and patience
sustain us one and all.*

*Please see us through our troubles,
the ones we face each day,
and feed us when we're hungry—
don't ever let us stray.*

God Began a Work in Me

"Being confident of this very thing,
that he which hath begun a good work in you
will perform it until the day of Jesus Christ."
(Philippians 1:6, KJV)

God began a work in me
that helps me grow in grace
and He will see this project through
until we're face-to-face.

The Lord Knows and Sees

The Lord is most wise—He knows and sees all—there is nothing humanity can hide from Him—not even the darkness can conceal us from the eyes of God.

"O LORD, thou hast searched me, and known me . . . Yea, the darkness hideth not from thee; but the night shineth as the day: the darkness and the light are both alike to thee."
(Psalm 139:1, 12, KJV)

*The Lord is our Shield,
our Maker and Guide.
He knows where we are,
from Him we can't hide.*

*He sees our true hearts
and knows every thought.
God understands us
and all of our faults.*

Keep Yourself in God's Love

"Keep yourselves in the love of God,
looking for the mercy of our Lord Jesus Christ
unto eternal life."
(Jude 1:21, KJV)

Lord, help us to remain within the boundaries of Your love throughout each day, and lead us upon the path to eternal life—embrace and transform us while we await our Savior's return.

*Keep us in Your boundaries
of love throughout each day,
our hearts long for Your presence—
don't keep us far away.*

*Please mold us and embrace us
while we await Your Son.
Prepare us for His Coming,
we ask that this be done.*

*Come guide us to the pathway
that leads to evermore,
the pathway to Your Kingdom . . .
in Christ's name we implore.*

Glory Hallelujah Lord

"By the word of the LORD were the heavens made;
and all the host of them by the breath of his mouth."
(Psalm 33:6, KJV)

*When stars come out at nighttime
and angels start to sing
God's glory shines from Heaven—
a blessing from our King.*

*Through darkened skies lights twinkle,
the moon shines in its place.
It's where the good Lord placed it
with His amazing grace.*

*O, glory, glory, glory,
to God, our righteous King,
the earth sings "hallelujah"
with every living thing.*

*In harmony we gather
to give Him thanks this day
and praise Him in the heavens
for His works and wondrous Way.*

"Sing unto God, ye kingdoms of the earth;
O sing praises unto the Lord . . . Sing unto him,
sing psalms unto him, talk ye of all his wondrous works.
Glory ye in his holy name."
(Psalm 68:32, 1 Chronicles 16:9–10, KJV)

I Poured My Heart Out

*I poured my heart out to the Lord,
nothing did I hide.
I told Him of my pain and fears . . .
things I'd kept inside.*

*He listened to each word I said
and did not turn from me.
Instead, He filled my soul with peace
and my heart with glee.*

Why Have You Forsaken Me?

"My God, my God, why hast thou forsaken me?"
(Matthew 27:46, KJV)

*God sacrificed His precious Son
so we could be set free.
He poured our sins into the One
that died for you and me.*

It was when our sins were poured into Jesus that He became separated from His Father. This caused our Savior to cry out in agonizing pain. The separation gripped His heart and wrenched His soul, yet, He remained obedient to God the Father, and sacrificed Himself for us.

*So, why did God forsake His Son
and cause His Lamb to cry?
It was because Christ bore our sins
that gave God reason why.*

*The Lord detests all wickedness,
it makes Him turn away.
And that is why He sent His wrath
on Jesus Christ that day . . .*

And then it was finished. Christ took our place on the cross—He "paid the price"—to pay our debt in full, thus allowing us to come into the presence of God's grace.

Forget the Past

"Remember ye not the former things,
neither consider the things of old.
Behold, I will do a new thing."
(Isaiah 43:18–19, KJV)

*Forget the past and start anew
don't dwell on things you can't undo.*

Be mindful that . . .

*Each brand new day God gives to you
is filled with hope and blessings too.*

A Special Gift

*God blessed me with a special gift,
a mom He gave to me.
He filled her with such tenderness
and generosity.*

*He mixed in love and lots of joy
and then a touch of grace.
He added hope and faithfulness
and kissed her dear, sweet face.*

*God stirred in trust and truthfulness
and gifts of honor, too.
He mixed them with humility
and blended in virtue.*

I Stand at the Door and Knock

"Behold, I stand at the door, and knock:
if any man hear my voice,
and open the door,
I will come in to him,
and will sup with him,
and he with me."
(Revelation 3:20, KJV)

*I stand at your door
and knock with great love
hoping you'll answer
My call from above.*

*I patiently wait
to see your sweet face
and grant you blessings
of favor and grace.*

Yesterday – Today – Tomorrow

*O, yesterday has come and gone,
its memories in the past.
Today was once a yesterday,
'twas a day that did not last.*

*Now, tomorrow is awaiting
and heading toward today,
and when that day comes to an end,
'twill become a yesterday.*

Bring an End to Wickedness

"Oh let the wickedness of the wicked come to an end;
but establish the just:
for the righteous God trieth the hearts and reins."
(Psalm 7:9, KJV)

*The world is filled with wickedness
in search of souls to own.
O, Father God, Almighty King,
come make our hearts Your home.*

*Protect us from the evil one,
O, precious Lord, above.
Explore our minds and hearts, dear God,
and fill us with Your love.*

*Come put an end to violence
and stop all wicked plans.
Please make the world a better place
for woman and for man.*

Keep Your Tongue from Evil

Lord,

*Please bless our mouths
and all we say
we need Your help
throughout each day.*

*"Keep thy tongue from evil,
and thy lips from speaking guile."
(Psalm 34:13, KJV)*

*Keep your tongue from evil
and lips from speaking lies.
Let your words be truthful,
not filled with compromise.*

Dwell Between His Shoulders

"The beloved of the LORD shall dwell in safety by him;
and the LORD shall cover him all the day long,
and he shall dwell between his shoulders."
(Deuteronomy 33:12, KJV)

*I dwell between the shoulders
of Almighty God above.
He keeps me safe from darkness
and protects me with His love.*

*So, who can ever harm me
when I'm with my Lord each day,
and tracking every footprint
He provides on my pathway?*

"And who is he that will harm you,
if ye be followers of that which is good?"
(1 Peter 3:13, KJV)

A Bouquet of Cheerful Joy

*I'm sending you this message,
a bouquet of joyful cheer,
in hopes that you will be blessed
every day throughout the year.*

*This sweet bouquet is special
'cause it overflows with love
and it's wrapped up in God's peace
with His mercy from above.*

*I pray this gift brings smiles
to your sweet, angelic face
and fills you with such gladness
and the blessings of God's grace.*

When a Man is a Slave

"For of whom a man is overcome,
of the same is he brought in bondage."
(2 Peter 2:19, KJV)

*When a man is a slave
to what masters him,
he entangles himself
in a world that's grim.*

*His soul is in bondage,
it's bargained away,
and oppressed he will be
'til he changes his way.*

*But the man who submits
to our mighty King
will be graced by riches
and blessings He brings.*

God's Plans for Me

"Boast not thyself of to morrow;
for thou knowest not what a day may bring forth."
(Proverbs 27:1, KJV)

*I boast not of tomorrow
for I know not of the plans
the good Lord fashioned for me,
as all things are in His hands.*

*It's He who holds my future,
only He knows what's to be.
No, I've not been made aware
of the plans God has for me.*

Jealousy and Selfishness

"But if ye have bitter envying and strife in your hearts,
glory not, and lie not against the truth.
This wisdom descendeth not from above,
but is earthly, sensual, devilish.
For where envying and strife is,
there is confusion and every evil work."
(James 3:14–16, KJV)

*Jealousy and selfishness
each lead us into sin,
inspired by the devil,
who's filled with evil whims.*

When We Acknowledge Him

"In all thy ways acknowledge him,
and he shall direct thy paths."
(Proverbs 3:6, KJV)

*When following a broken path
and cannot find your way,
just lean upon Almighty God
and you'll no longer stray.*

*The Lord will be the Guiding Light
that sets your pathway straight.
Come place your faith and hope in Him;
with open arms He waits.*

*Abundantly He'll change your life
and you'll find peace within.
Your eyes will see, and ears will hear
when you acknowledge Him.*

Listen for the Voice of God

"Iniquities prevail against me:
as for our transgressions, thou shalt purge them away."
(Psalm 65:3, KJV)

*No matter what you've said or done
God hears and sees it all.
He comes to you with love and grace
to lift you when you fall.*

*He washes you of darkened sins
that stain with ugliness,
and He does not keep a diary
of sins you have confessed.*

*So, listen for the voice of God,
He's calling out your name.
He calls to give you blessings,
not worldly things or fame.*

The Lord Delights

"I am the LORD which exercise lovingkindness,
judgment, and righteousness, in the earth:
for in these things I delight, saith the LORD."
(Jeremiah 9:24, KJV)

*The Lord delights in righteousness,
faith, and honesty,
and wants us to show kindness
with love, collectively.*

Weary and Burdened

"Take my yoke upon you, and learn of me;
for I am meek and lowly in heart:
and ye shall find rest unto your souls.
For my yoke is easy, and my burden is light."
(Matthew 11:29–30, KJV)

*We come to You with heavy hearts
to seek Your shining face
in hopes You'll give us rest, dear Lord,
and bless us with Your grace.*

*Please take our yokes that weigh us down
and make our burdens light.
We trust You, Lord, with all our cares
and ask You make things right.*

Creation Proclaims

"Who maketh the clouds his chariot;
Who walketh upon the wings of the wind;
Who maketh winds his messengers."
(Psalm 104:3–4, ASV)

As the winds blow softly
throughout all the land
they carry a message
of One truly grand.

Declaring God's glory
and works of His hand,
all of Creation
proclaims the Lord's Plan.

"The heavens declare the glory of God;
And the firmament showeth his handiwork."
(Psalm 19:1, ASV)

Eyes You Granted Me

Lord,

*Today I came to rest
and spent my day with You.
It was only then
my eyes had a clear view . . .*

*I witnessed worldly things
diminish from my sight.
They were all replaced
by the glory of Your Light.*

*Through eyes of faith I saw
what this world can't see . . .
beauty through Your eyes—
eyes You granted me.*

Our Savior's Gift

"And, behold, the veil of the temple was rent in twain
from the top to the bottom; and the earth did quake,
and the rocks rent."
(Matthew 27:51, KJV)

*The Prince of Peace . . . a Crown of Glory . . .
unselfish deeds, all tell His story . . .*

*The Lamb of God . . . the Son of Man . . .
bearing scars on feet and hands.*

*The veil was torn . . . the earth did quake . . .
Christ gave His life for all our sakes.*

*Our Savior's Gift . . . redeeming love . . .
forgiven sins by God above . . .*

*O, Jesus Christ, sweet King of kings,
we give You thanks for everything.*

What Good Will It Be?

"For what is a man profited,
if he shall gain the whole world, and lose his own soul?
or what shall a man give in exchange for his soul?"
(Matthew 16:26, KJV)

*What good will it be for man to gain
the entire world as his own,
while losing his soul in the taking
and turning his heart to stone?*

The Hand of God

"I waited patiently for the LORD; and he inclined unto me,
and heard my cry. He brought me up also out of an horrible pit,
out of the miry clay, and set my feet upon a rock,
and established my goings.
And he hath put a new song in my mouth,
even praise unto our God: many shall see it, and fear,
and shall trust in the LORD."
(Psalm 40:1–3, KJV)

One day I met a man
who cried out in distress.
He said he was ashamed
and wanted to confess.

He got down on his knees
and prayed to God above,
"Lord, I want forgiveness,
but don't deserve Your love."

He looked back on his past
and all the evil things
that led him where he'd been,
away from God, our King.

He'd faced some troubled times,
alone, not trusting God,
and traveled to a place
where sinful folks had trod.

He'd walked there on his own,
away from Yahweh's Light,
as darkness captured him
and held him day and night.

The place unleashed its sin
and caused his heart to fear.
This site was dark and grim
which made his view unclear.

He shouted out to God
as tears flowed from his eyes.
He asked for clemency,
in anguish did he cry.

The Lord had heard his plea
and to his side He came.
The man confessed each sin
and had no one to blame.

'Twas then the good Lord reached
with His extended arms
and drew this man to Him
to save his soul from harm.

Clothe Us

"Put on therefore, as the elect of God, holy and beloved,
bowels of mercies, kindness, humbleness of mind, meekness,
longsuffering; Forbearing one another, and forgiving one another,
if any man have a quarrel against any:
even as Christ forgave you, so also do ye.
And above all these things put on charity,
which is the bond of perfectness."
(Colossians 3:12–14, KJV)

Clothe us in a wardrobe
of patience, love, and grace.
Help us share Your kindness
with each one that we face.

Bless us with compassion,
humility, and peace.
Grant us willing spirits
that won't let faith decrease.

Give to us discernment,
don't let us be deceived.
Fill us with Your Truth, Lord,
and help us to believe.

Bind us with perfection
secured with charity.
Sprinkle gifts of mercy
with generosity.

Teach us Your forgiveness
and faithful, gentle Ways.
Take us by the hand, Lord,
and usher us each day.

Steadfast Feet

"How beautiful upon the mountains
are the feet of him that bringeth good tidings,
that publisheth peace;
that bringeth good tidings of good,
that publisheth salvation."
(Isaiah 52:7, KJV)

Lord, bless me with steadfast feet—ones that will not stumble when confronted by obstacles. Allow them to be quick when dodging the enemy, and diligent when carrying me to share Your Good News with others. Let nothing prevent me from spreading Your Word.

*Bless me, Lord, with steadfast feet
that carry me each day.
Help me spread Your mighty Word
to those who've gone astray.*

*I want to share Your Good News
so others will know too
the joyful peace and saving grace
that only come from You.*

Bless the Children

"He shall cover thee with his feathers,
and under his wings shalt thou trust:
his truth shall be thy shield and buckler."
(Psalm 91:4, KJV)

*Lord, bless the children of this world,
keep them safe and sound.
Don't let the devil capture them
and keep them ever bound.*

*Protect their tender innocence,
don't let them shake with fear.
Come shelter them beneath Your wing
where they'll be safe and near.*

I Love Those Who Love Me

"I love them that love me;
and those that seek me early shall find me."
(Proverbs 8:17, KJV)

*I love those who love Me
and seek Me each day.
I love those who draw near
and won't turn away.*

*Come find Me, My children,
I'm very close by.
Come search with your hearts
and behold the Most High.*

Grace and Peace

"Grace be to you and peace from God our Father,
and from the Lord Jesus Christ."
(2 Corinthians 1:2, KJV)

*God blessed me with such precious gifts
I'd like to share with you.
He wrapped them in His perfect peace
and told me what to do.*

*"Come give My gifts of love and grace
to those you meet each day
and do not keep them for yourself,
they're meant to give away."*

So, in obedience . . .

*I come to share God's gifts with you
and pray you'll share them too.
It's when you give these gifts away
more blessings come to you.*

Jesus Helps Those Tempted

"For in that he himself hath suffered being tempted,
he is able to succour them that are tempted."
(Hebrews 2:18, KJV)

*Jesus knows the suffering
each one of us goes through
and He knows how Satan tempts
the souls that he pursues.*

*Christ withstood each given test
that Satan put Him through
and He'll guide each one of us
when we are tempted too.*

*We just need to ask for help
with trials that we face
and Christ will gladly lead us
with mercy, love, and grace.*

I Cried to the Lord

"I waited patiently for the LORD;
and he inclined unto me, and heard my cry.
He brought me up also out of an horrible pit,
out of the miry clay, and set my feet upon a rock,
and established my goings."
(Psalm 40:1–2, KJV)

*I cried to the Lord in hopeless despair
and dropped to my knees in tearful prayer.
He listened. He heard. He knew of my pain.
God lifted me up from where I'd been slain.*

*He steadied my feet as I walked along.
He guided my steps and helped me grow strong.
God blessed me with joy and filled me with grace.
I felt the Lord's love and gentle embrace.*

"And he hath put a new song in my mouth,
even praise unto our God."
(Psalm 40:3, KJV)

*I sing to the Lord
with praises all days
and give Him my thanks
for His gracious ways.*

Many Will Come to Deceive

"Take heed lest any man deceive you:
For many shall come in my name,
saying, I am Christ; and shall deceive many."
(Mark 13:5–6, KJV)

*So many will come
in the name of the Lord
deceiving mankind
with a double-edged sword.*

*The words they will speak
will proclaim, "I am He,"
but those who know God
will believe that can't be.*

The Lord is Our Shepherd

"The LORD is my shepherd."
(Psalm 23:1, KJV)

*The Lord is our Shepherd
and into the light
He leads us from darkness
all days and each night.*

*Christ shields us from danger
beneath His great wing
where we are secluded
from all evil things.*

*With Christ as our Shepherd
there's nothing to fear.
He is a strong tower
forever revered.*

Satan is a Prowler

"Your adversary the devil, as a roaring lion,
walketh about, seeking whom he may devour."
(1 Peter 5:8, KJV)

*Satan is a prowler
who searches for his prey.
He roars like a lion
in hopes to get his way.*

*Resist his temptations,
do not adhere to him.
He will only lead you
to a place that is grim.*

*He's ruthless and evil
and he wants you to stray.
Don't let him entice you,
pray the devil away.*

"Submit yourselves therefore to God.
Resist the devil, and he will flee from you."
(James 4:7, KJV)

*Submit yourself to God
and pray to Him each day.
Ask the Lord to send
the devil on his way . . .*

*It's when you trust in God
and follow only He
that Satan will withdraw—
he'll flee and let you be.*

Don't be Misled

"And he said, Take heed that ye be not deceived:
for many shall come in my name, saying, I am Christ;
and the time draweth near: go ye not therefore after them . . .
And there shall be signs in the sun, and in the moon, and in the stars;
and upon the earth distress of nations, with perplexity; the sea
and the waves roaring; Men's hearts failing them for fear,
and for looking after those things which are coming on the earth:
for the powers of heaven shall be shaken. And then shall they see
the Son of man coming in a cloud with power and great glory.
And when these things begin to come to pass, then look up,
and lift up your heads; for your redemption draweth nigh."
(Luke 21:8, 25–28, KJV)

*Many shall come in godly disguise
and try to deceive with misleading lies.
Do not believe, they'll lead you astray.
These things will take place near Judgment Day.*

*Strange things will appear throughout the skies,
significant warnings seen by all eyes.
Omens of evil, portents above,
all will be warnings from our God of love.*

*Dismay on the earth will try all mankind,
fear will run rampant confusing the mind.
Perplexed by these signs, many will flee,
and oceans will rage with intensity.*

*The courage of some may falter and fail.
Fear of their fate will cause them to wail.
The Day is forthcoming, time does draws near,
these things will take place 'fore Jesus appears.*

Implant Your Truth in Our Hearts

"Shew me thy ways, O LORD; teach me thy paths.
Lead me in thy truth, and teach me:
for thou art the God of my salvation;
on thee do I wait all the day.
Remember, O LORD, thy tender mercies
and thy lovingkindnesses;
for they have been ever of old."
(Psalm 25:4–6, KJV)

Lord,

*Implant Your Truth in our hearts
and let the roots grow deep.
Fill us with integrity
and grant us all safekeep.*

*Shepherd us with tender care,
please lead us with Your love.
Guide us on Your narrow path
on wings of mourning doves.*

*Embrace us with Your mercy
and let Your voice be heard.
Open up our hearts and souls
and fill us with Your Word.*

I Didn't Have a Choice

"Ye have not chosen me, but I have chosen you."
(John 15:16, KJV)

*Christ Jesus chose to love me,
I did not have a choice.
He thought I was worth saving . . .
O, how I rejoice.*

God's Peace

"Peace I leave with you, my peace I give unto you:
not as the world giveth, give I unto you.
Let not your heart be troubled, neither let it be afraid."
(John 14:27, KJV)

*The peace that Yahweh offers
isn't of this place.
It's from His mighty Kingdom
given with His grace.*

So . . .

*Don't be troubled, nor afraid,
let your soul rejoice.
Come sing with joy, and go in peace,
listen for God's voice.*

"For ye shall go out with joy, and be led forth with peace."
(Isaiah 55:12, KJV)

I Wandered Through a Valley

"Oh that I were as in months past,
as in the days when God preserved me;
When his candle shined upon my head,
and when by his light I walked through darkness."
(Job 29:2–3, KJV)

*I wandered through a valley
where I could barely see.
Yahweh knew that I was lost
and came to rescue me.*

*He led me from the darkness
onto a narrow path
and then upon a mountain,
no place was there for wrath.*

*'Twas then my eyes were opened
and I began to see . . .
God shined His Glory on me—
the Lord had set me free.*

One Day in His Courts

"For a day in thy courts is better than a thousand."
(Psalm 84:10, KJV)

*I stand in awe before the Lord,
in silence I am still.
I listen with an open heart
in hopes to learn His Will.*

*My soul is wrapped in perfect peace,
God's mercy knows no bounds.
I'm bathed in His amazing grace,
His glory I have found.*

*My thirsty spirit is now quenched
by God's unending love.
My heart is wrapped in loving arms,
the arms of God above.*

*The good Lord brought me to this place
because He heard my prayer.
I'd asked for one day in His Courts,
that's why He brought me there.*

Jesus Set Me Free

"If the Son therefore shall make you free,
ye shall be free indeed."
(John 8:36, KJV)

*I close my eyes and listen,
there's nothing I can see.
I wait to hear the whisper
of Jesus calling me.*

*And as I wait in stillness
I bow on bended knee
praising my sweet Savior
for all He's done for me.*

*It's then I hear Christ Jesus
who's whispering to me,
with angels in the background
singing beautifully.*

*Although my eyes can't see Him
I know He's here with me.
His presence is so peaceful
and ever heavenly . . .*

*My heart sings out with gladness
as Jesus sets me free
of all the heavy burdens
that once imprisoned me.*

A Righteous Path

"He maketh me to lie down in green pastures:
he leadeth me beside the still waters.
He restoreth my soul:
he leadeth me in the paths of righteousness
for his name's sake."
(Psalm 23:2–3, KJV)

*I walk upon a righteous path
designed by God, with love.
I listen to so many sounds
and songs of turtledoves.*

*God leads me to His tranquil grounds
and guards my soul from harm.
It's there my spirit is refreshed
while resting in His arms.*

*My heart has come to know God's peace,
a peace that's truly pure,
and as I bask in His sweet love
I'm blessed forevermore.*

Be Still

"Be still, and know that I am God."
(Psalm 46:10, KJV)

*"Be still, My child, and know that I'm God,
don't follow the path where many have trod.*

*Come rest beside Me and quiet your soul.
Trust in Me always, relinquish control.*

*I'll show you a path that I have designed
for all your travels, and all of mankind.*

*The journey is marked with signs from My Son
who gave of Himself to save everyone.*

*He came before you so none would be lost
and paved a pathway, at a severe cost.*

*A battle He fought—a battle He won—
the ransom was paid, and the deed was done."*

"For Christ also hath once suffered for sins,
the just for the unjust,
that he might bring us to God,
being put to death in the flesh,
but quickened by the Spirit."
(1 Peter 3:18, KJV)

Ask – Seek – Knock

"Ask, and it shall be given you;
seek, and ye shall find;
knock, and it shall be opened unto you:
For every one that asketh receiveth;
and he that seeketh findeth;
and to him that knocketh it shall be opened."
(Matthew 7:7–8, KJV)

*For all who ask they shall receive
and those who seek shall find.
And they that knock upon the door
shall find our God Divine.*

Home

"Ask, and it shall be given you...
For every one that asketh receiveth."
(Matthew 7:7–8, KJV)

*There are several steppingstones
to choose that lead us Home
and if we do not ask God's help
haphazardly we'll roam.*

"Enter ye in at the strait gate: for wide is the gate,
and broad is the way, that leadeth to destruction,
and many there be which go in thereat:
Because strait is the gate, and narrow is the way,
which leadeth unto life, and few there be that find it . . .
Verily I say unto you, Except ye be converted,
and become as little children,
ye shall not enter into the kingdom of heaven,"
(Matthew 7:13–14, 18:3, KJV).

*Christ has made it possible
to kneel before God's Throne
and pray that He'll reveal to us
the stones that lead us Home.*

*Our Savior also whispers,
"Your pride you must disown
and become like little ones
before you travel Home."*

Lead Us from the Evil One

"And lead us not into temptation,
but deliver us from evil."
(Matthew 6:13, KJV)

Dear Lord,

*Lead us from the evil one
to Your hallowed grounds.
Bless the people of this world
with love that knows no bounds.*

We Knock at the Door

"I will feed my flock, and I will cause them to lie down,
saith the Lord God. I will seek that which was lost,
and bring again that which was driven away,
and will bind up that which was broken,
and will strengthen that which was sick."
(Ezekiel 34:15–16, KJV)

We knock at the door of mercy
while on our knees in prayer.
We call out Your name, good Shepherd,
in a moment of great despair.

We wandered far from Your presence.
Come find us for we have all strayed.
We're lost in a world of darkness;
we've scattered and can't find our way.

Please lead us back to Your fold, Christ,
and bring us to safe, tranquil grounds.
We long to lie down in Your peace
but can't 'til we all have been found.

Come shepherd us, precious Jesus,
so never again do we stray.
We've made mistakes and we're sorry.
Don't leave us to find our own way.

"Of them which thou gavest me have I lost none."
(John 18:9, KJV)

Yahweh Whispers to My Heart

*Yahweh whispers to my heart
and wants me to draw near
but when I am distracted
sometimes I do not hear.*

*It's when I do not listen
and do things my own way
I learn a costly lesson
with each time that I stray.*

*I want no more distractions
so I may hear God's voice
and each word that He whispers . . .
O, how I'd rejoice.*

Now . . .

*I come to You, my Father,
and pray You take control
of all my words and actions
and all my heart and soul.*

I Listened to the Quiet

"And God saw every thing that he had made,
and, behold, it was very good."
(Genesis 1:31, KJV)

*I listened to the quiet
and stillness of the day,
a day that was created
in Yahweh's perfect Way.*

*The sun was slowly rising
extending bright, warm rays,
reaching out to all on Earth
this blessed, perfect day.*

*The sleepy earth awakened
and birds began to sing
giving thanks and praise to God,
the Maker of all things.*

*And as the day moved onward
the sun began to set.
God looked down from the heavens
and saw each need was met.*

Bring Me to My Knees

"Humble yourselves in the sight of the Lord,
and he shall lift you up."
(James 4:10, KJV)

*Bring me to my knees, dear Lord,
and make me humble too.
Cleanse me of my wrongful deeds,
the old ones and the new.*

*Change my heart and make it pure,
unveil my eyes to see.
Lift me up, Almighty God,
please hear my humble plea.*

Come One, Come All

"I will praise thee, O LORD, with my whole heart;
I will shew forth all thy marvellous works.
I will be glad and rejoice in thee:
I will sing praise to thy name, O thou most High."
(Psalm 9:1–2, KJV)

*Come one, come all, to praise the Lord,
rejoice in God above.
Kneel before our mighty King
and worship Him with love.*

*Pray to God with all your heart
and deep within your soul.
Seek His face and you'll be blessed
as each new day unfolds.*

*Give thanks to God, for He is Lord,
tell of His wondrous deeds.
Come rejoice, delight in Him,
proclaim that you've been freed.*

The Day of the Lord

"Blow ye the trumpet in Zion,
and sound an alarm in my holy mountain:
let all the inhabitants of the land tremble:
for the day of the LORD cometh, for it is nigh at hand . . .
And it shall come to pass afterward, that I will pour out my spirit
upon all flesh; and your sons and your daughters shall prophesy,
your old men shall dream dreams, your young men shall see visions . . .
And I will shew wonders in the heavens and
in the earth, blood, and fire, and pillars of smoke.
The sun shall be turned into darkness, and the moon into blood,
before the great and terrible day of the LORD come.
And it shall come to pass, that whosoever shall call
on the name of the LORD shall be delivered: for in mount Zion
and in Jerusalem shall be deliverance, as the LORD hath said,
and in the remnant whom the LORD shall call."
(Joel 2:1, 28, 30–32, KJV)

A trumpet will blast a warning
and it will be heard by all.
Locusts will swarm over regions,
they'll charge through lands and scale walls.

The Day of the Lord is coming
and children will prophesy.
Young men will see many visions,
strange things will rise in the sky.

The Lord will pour out His Spirit,
old men will come to dream dreams.
The Day will soon be upon us
when Christ will claim the redeemed.

The sun will be turned to darkness
'fore this great and awful Day.
Come give your hearts to Lord Jesus,
turn to Him, repent, and pray.

The Gift He Sent My Way

"Every good gift and every perfect gift is from above,
and cometh down from the Father of lights,
with whom is no variableness, neither shadow of turning."
(James 1:17, KJV)

*One day while I was walking, I found a winding trail.
Its beauty was astounding, perfection was detailed.*

*And as I traveled onward, a peace came over me,
it moved within my spirit so ever joyfully.*

*'Twas then my ears heard something. I turned my head to see
a stately waterfall cascading gracefully.*

*I stood there in amazement and listened to its sounds
watching every movement of water splashing down.*

*The sight was captivating, a peaceful, calming view.
It was exhilarating—I truly felt renewed.*

*I thanked the Lord, my Father, for blessing me this day
and praised Him for this rare gift that He had sent my way.*

My Heart is Filled with Gratitude

"Offer unto God thanksgiving;
and pay thy vows unto the most High."
(Psalm 50:14, KJV)

*There are countless things in life
that we are thankful for.
Our hearts are filled with gratitude
for blessings from You, Lord.*

*And now we lift a joyful song
on wings of turtle doves
to praise You, Lord, Almighty God,
with gratitude and love.*

"Let us come before his presence with thanksgiving,
and make a joyful noise unto him with psalms."
(Psalm 95:2, KJV)

The Valley of Despair

"I waited patiently for the LORD;
and he inclined unto me, and heard my cry.
He brought me up also out of an horrible pit,
out of the miry clay, and set my feet upon a rock,
and established my goings.
And he hath put a new song in my mouth,
even praise unto our God: many shall see it, and fear,
and shall trust in the LORD."
(Psalm 40:1–3, KJV)

As I walked into the valley, the valley of despair,
my soul cried out to Yahweh, "This truly is unfair."

The Lord had heard me calling, He heard my frightened plea.
'Twas then I heard Him whisper, "Be still and rest with Me.

My child, I'll never leave you, sometimes you leave My side,
and think that I don't see you, although you try to hide.

I know you are in trouble and need My help this day.
Come grasp My hand, I'm reaching, so you can find your way.

I'll lift you from the mire, deep down in that dark pit,
and set your feet upon a rock, where you may rest a bit.

I'll give to you a new song, a hymn of praise to Me,
a song that tells the story of how I set you free."

"For he hath not despised nor abhorred
the affliction of the afflicted;
neither hath he hid his face from him;
but when he cried unto him, he heard."
(Psalm 22:24, KJV)

Turn Darkness to Light

*I see and I listen
to all the world's news
and pray to You, Yahweh,
for all that I view.*

*There's famine and sickness,
and hurricanes too.
So many are hurting,
trying to make do.*

*Please come to awaken
Your joy in their hearts
and bless them with mercy
as each new day starts.*

*Place smiles on faces,
let no one be shunned.
Feed the world with Your love
and that of Your Son.*

*Bring peace to all nations
as each one unites.
Give strength to Your children,
turn darkness to Light.*

The Hands and Feet of Christ

"For if they fall, the one will lift up his fellow."
(Ecclesiastes 4:10, KJV)

*Lord, I see faces wrought with pain,
the suffering, intense.
I know not what they're going through
but know it is immense.*

*I want to lend a helping hand
to ease their pain and tears.
I ask You, Lord, "What can I do?
Please speak so I may hear.*

*I pray to be the hands and feet
of Jesus Christ, Your Son.
Enable me, Almighty God,
so I may help someone."*

Commit to God

"Commit thy works unto the LORD,
and thy thoughts shall be established."
(Proverbs 16:3, KJV)

*Commit to God in all you do
and He will bless your plans.
Place all your trust in God above,
leave all things in His hands.*

Gathered Burdens

"Come unto me, all ye that labor and are heavy laden,
and I will give you rest.
Take my yoke upon you, and learn of me;
for I am meek and lowly in heart:
and ye shall find rest unto your souls.
For my yoke is easy, and my burden is light."
(Matthew 11:28–30, KJV)

*I've gathered many burdens
along the path of life
and do not wish to keep them,
they've caused me so much strife.*

*My yoke is far too heavy
to carry one more night.
My life is dark and dreary
and I cannot see Your Light.*

*Please show me where You are, Lord,
I want to meet with You
to give You all my burdens
and bid them all adieu.*

Dine with the Lord

Lord,

*Gather people, lost and least,
around Your table for a feast.
Have them dine on hope and grace
with lovely linens made of lace.*

*Fill their hearts with faithfulness
and wash away their weariness.
Serve them helpings of Your peace,
all those invited to the feast.*

*Bring their cups to overflow
with seeds of love and help them grow.
Bless each one this very day
and let not one be turned away.*

God's Glory

"And ye said, Behold, the LORD our God
hath shewed us his glory and his greatness."
(Deuteronomy 5:24, KJV)

*May the glory of God
and that of His Son
shine down on the earth
and bless everyone.*

Equip Us with Your Armor

"Be strong in the Lord . . . Put on the whole armour of God,
that ye may be able to stand against the wiles of the devil . . .
Stand therefore, having your loins girt about with truth,
and having on the breastplate of righteousness; And your feet shod
with the preparation of the gospel of peace; Above all,
taking the shield of faith, wherewith ye shall be able to quench
all the fiery darts of the wicked. And take the helmet of salvation,
and the sword of the Spirit, which is the word of God."
(Ephesians 6:10–11, 14–17, KJV)

Adorn us in Your armor
and keep us safe each day.
Protect us from all evil
so we don't go astray.

Equip us with the helmet
that Your salvation brings.
Wrap Your truth around us, Lord,
and buckle it, dear King.

Come dress us in the breastplate
of strength and righteousness.
Lord, fit our feet with footwear
that takes us to wit-ness.

Give to us a mighty shield
of faith, and honor too,
so that we're protected, Lord,
from all that's not of You.

Etch Your Word upon us, God,
and give to us Your Sword
so we may slay the devil
and glorify You, Lord.

He Knows What's in Your Heart

"Grant thee according to thine own heart,
and fulfill all thy counsel."
(Psalm 20:4, KJV)

*The good Lord knows what's in your heart:
your hopes, your dreams, desires.
I pray to God in Jesus' name
that each one be acquired.*

Quenching Rains

"In the wilderness shall waters break out,
and streams in the desert.
And the parched ground shall become a pool,
and the thirsty land springs of water."
(Isaiah 35:6–7, KJV)

*I hear thunder roaring
while raging through the skies,
as lightning strikes through clouds
before my very eyes.*

*The earth is dry and waiting
to welcome quenching rains
as riverbanks diminish
and droughts come stake their claim.*

*All life on Earth cries out
and prays that God sends rain.
He hears its anguished plea
and takes away its pain.*

And then God sends His precious rains . . .

*Rain-filled clouds come bursting forth
in search of sun-scorched lands,
not holding back the moisture
from the good Lord's hands.*

The Seed of Loneliness

*Loneliness has sown itself
in hearts and minds this day.
Stop these seeds from growing, Lord,
through Jesus Christ I pray.*

"Mine eyes are ever toward the LORD;
for he shall pluck my feet out of the net. Turn thee unto me,
and have mercy upon me; for I am desolate and afflicted.
The troubles of my heart are enlarged:
O bring thou me out of my distresses."
(Psalm 25:15–17, KJV)

*May loneliness not find a way
to captivate your mind.
Don't let it take control of you,
leave loneliness behind.*

*Give God your seed of loneliness,
come leave it at His feet,
and trust Him with your heart and soul . . .
watch loneliness retreat.*

Now . . .

*Rejoice, be glad, before the Lord
as He rides upon the clouds.
Extol Him and His Holy Name,
come praise the Lord out loud.*

"Let the righteous be glad; let them rejoice before God:
yea, let them exceedingly rejoice. Sing unto God,
sing praises to his name: extol him that rideth upon
the heavens by his name JAH, and rejoice before him."
(Psalm 68:3–4, KJV)

I Lay My Heart Before You

"Submit yourselves therefore to God."
(James 4:7, KJV)

*I lay my heart before You
and render my soul too.
With faithfulness and trust, Lord,
I pledge my life to You.*

*I look to You for guidance
with every step I take,
and ask You grant me wisdom
for choices that I make.*

*With every complex notion
please make them simpler ones
and pave the way before me
with footprints from Your Son.*

*And while I'm on this journey,
please shelter me from harm.
O, lift me, Holy Father,
and hold me in Your arms.*

*Renew my soul and spirit,
come cleanse me from within.
Please give to me a pure heart
and wash away my sins.*

Amid the Quiet

*Amid the quiet
God whispered to me,
"I'm with you always,
although you can't see.*

*I made all the world
for all humankind
and gave sight to those
whose spirits were blind.*

*I love my children,
each one is so rare
and each was created
with sweet, loving care."*

Search My Heart and Soul

"O LORD, thou hast searched me, and known me.
Thou knowest my downsitting and mine uprising,
thou understandest my thought afar off.
Thou compassest my path and my lying down,
and art acquainted with all my ways.
For there is not a word in my tongue, but, lo, O LORD,
thou knowest it altogether.
Thou hast beset me behind and before,
and laid thine hand upon me . . .
Search me, O God, and know my heart:
try me, and know my thoughts:
And see if there be any wicked way in me,
and lead me in the way everlasting."
(Psalm 139:1–5, 23–24, KJV)

God sees the hearts of all mankind
and deep within each soul.
He understands our willful ways
and purpose of our goals.

There's nothing we can hide from Him,
He knows our thoughts and deeds.
The Lord is wise beyond all bounds
and knows our every need.

With this in mind, I humbly pray . . .

Please search my heart and soul, dear Lord,
I ask of You this day.
Come take my hand and show me, God,
Your everlasting way.

Rescued

"Grace to you and peace from God the Father,
and our Lord Jesus Christ, who gave himself for our sins,
that he might deliver us out of this present evil world."
(Galatians 1:3–4, ASV)

*My life had been a whirlwind
just spinning 'round and 'round.
My feet were always moving
but never touching ground.*

*My heart was ever searching,
for what, I did not know,
while something deep inside me
sparked life and made it grow.*

*I did not know exactly
what touched my inner core.
The feeling was unknown,
one I'd never felt before.*

*And then one day while praying
tears ran down my face
and all that I'd done wrong
was shown to me, with grace.*

*The Lord in all His glory
had come to rescue me
from a world of darkness
and helped my heart to see.*

*It's then I came to kneel down
to confess of my sins
as Jesus knelt beside me
and drew me close to Him.*

He said I was forgiven
for all wrongs I had done
because He fought the battle—
a battle He had won.

Seeds of Kindness

"The desire of a man is his kindness."
(Proverbs 19:22, KJV)

*Kindness is an act of love
made up of thoughtful deeds,
and when it's used to bless someone
those blessings birth more seeds.*

Whispered Prayers

Dear Lord,

*The prayers I lift to You with love
are whispered from my heart.
I trust You'll hear each one I pray—
each prayer that I impart . . .*

And now . . .

*I thank You, Lord, for listening
and bending down Your ear.
I thank You for acknowledging
each prayer that You do hear.*

Prayer

"Praying always with all prayer and supplication in the Spirit, and watching thereunto with all perseverance and supplication for all saints," (Ephesians 6:18, KJV).

"If my people, which are called by my name, shall humble themselves, and pray, and seek my face, and turn from their wicked ways; then will I hear from heaven," (2 Chronicles 7:14, KJV).

"The LORD hath heard my supplication; the LORD will receive my prayer," (Psalm 6:9, KJV).

"O thou that hearest prayer, unto thee shall all flesh come," (Psalm 65:2, KJV).

"Blessed be God, which hath not turned away my prayer, nor his mercy from me," (Psalm 66:20, KJV).

"And all things, whatsoever ye shall ask in prayer, believing, ye shall receive," (Matthew 21:22, KJV).

"Therefore I say unto you, What things soever ye desire, when ye pray, believe that ye receive them, and ye shall have them," (Mark 11:24, KJV).

"Continue in prayer, and watch in the same with thanksgiving," (Colossians 4:2, KJV).

"And he spake a parable unto them to this end, that men ought always to pray, and not to faint," (Luke 18:1, KJV).

"And I say unto you, Ask, and it shall be given you; seek, and ye shall find; knock, and it shall be opened unto you. For every one that asketh receiveth; and he that seeketh findeth; and to him that knocketh it shall be opened," (Luke 11: 9–10, KJV).

"He will regard the prayer of the destitute, and not despise their prayer," (Psalm 102:17, KJV).

"I love the LORD, because he hath heard my voice and my supplications. Because he hath inclined his ear unto me, therefore will I call upon him as long as I live," (Psalm 116:1–2, KJV).

Pray with All Your Heart

"He shall call upon me, and I will answer him."
(Psalm 91:15, KJV)

Pray to God with all your heart,
He'll hear your every word . . .
and if you choose to whisper,
your whispers will be heard.

With inclined ear He'll listen
and answer, in His time.
Be still and wait upon Him—
God has His own timeline.

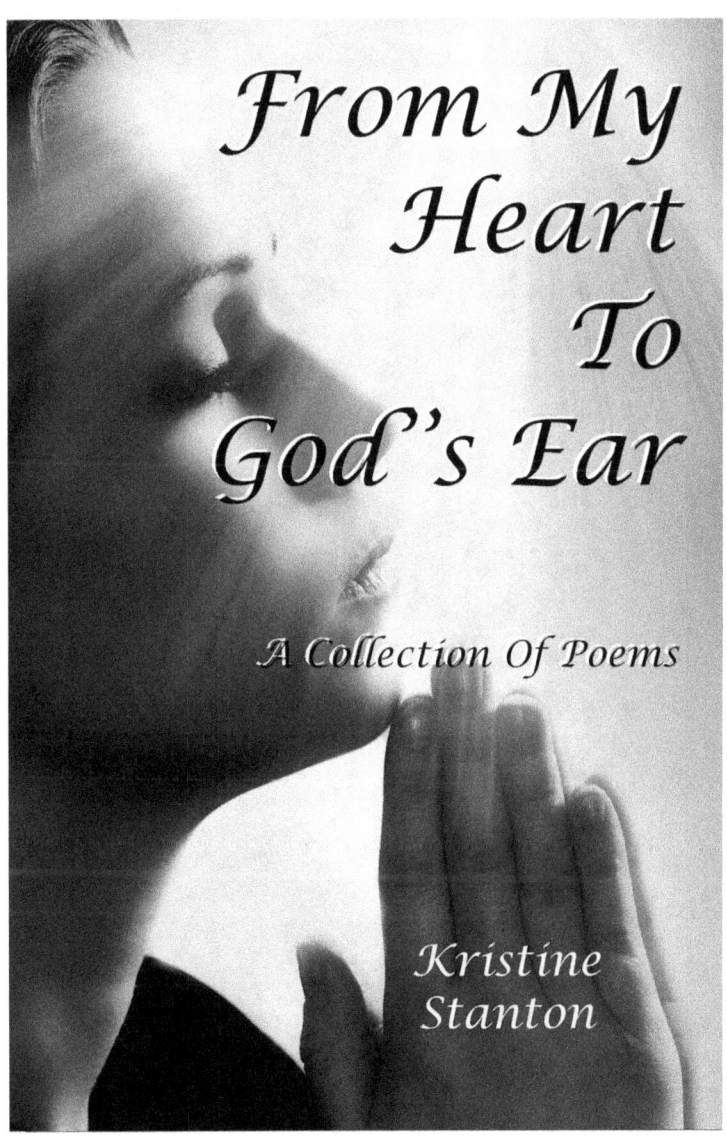

From My Heart To God's Ear – A Collection Of Poems
can be found on the following Amazon link:

https://www.amazon.com/s?k=kristine+stanton&ref=nb_sb_noss

www.ingramcontent.com/pod-product-compliance
Lightning Source LLC
Chambersburg PA
CBHW050320120526
44592CB00014B/1983